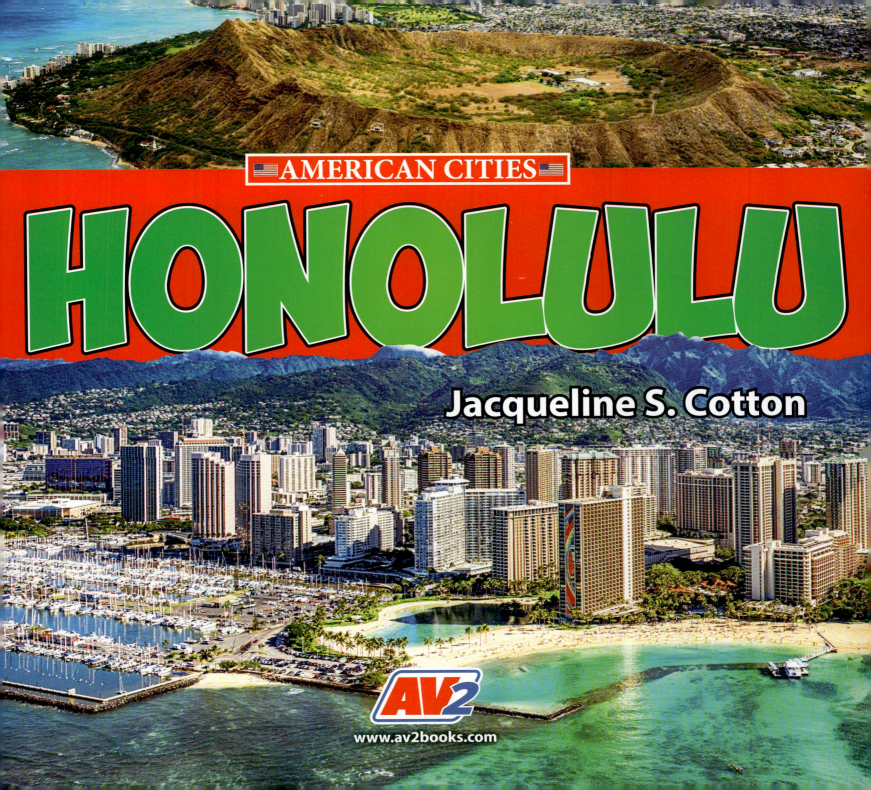

Step 1
Go to www.av2books.com

Step 2
Enter this unique code

XDLPBSO4Y

Step 3
Explore your interactive eBook!

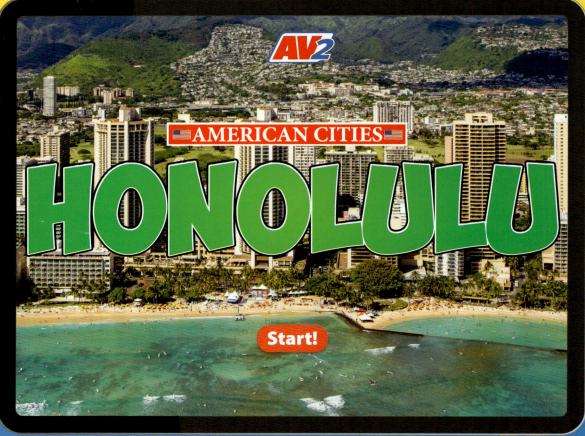

AMERICAN CITIES
HONOLULU
Start!

Your interactive eBook comes with...

AV2 is optimized for use on any device

Audio
Listen to the entire book read aloud

Videos
Watch informative video clips

Weblinks
Gain additional information for research

Try This!
Complete activities and hands-on experiments

Key Words
Study vocabulary, and complete a matching word activity

Quizzes
Test your knowledge

Slideshows
View images and captions

View new titles and product videos at www.av2books.com

Contents

- 2 AV2 Book Code
- 4 Get to Know Honolulu
- 6 Where Is Honolulu?
- 8 Climate
- 10 Population and Geography
- 12 Many Peoples
- 14 Tourism
- 16 Sports
- 18 Economy
- 20 Honolulu Timeline
- 22 Things to Do in Honolulu
- 24 Key Words

Get to Know
Honolulu

4

Honolulu is the capital city of Hawaii. It is known for its beautiful beaches. Waikiki Beach is one of the most popular beaches in the world.

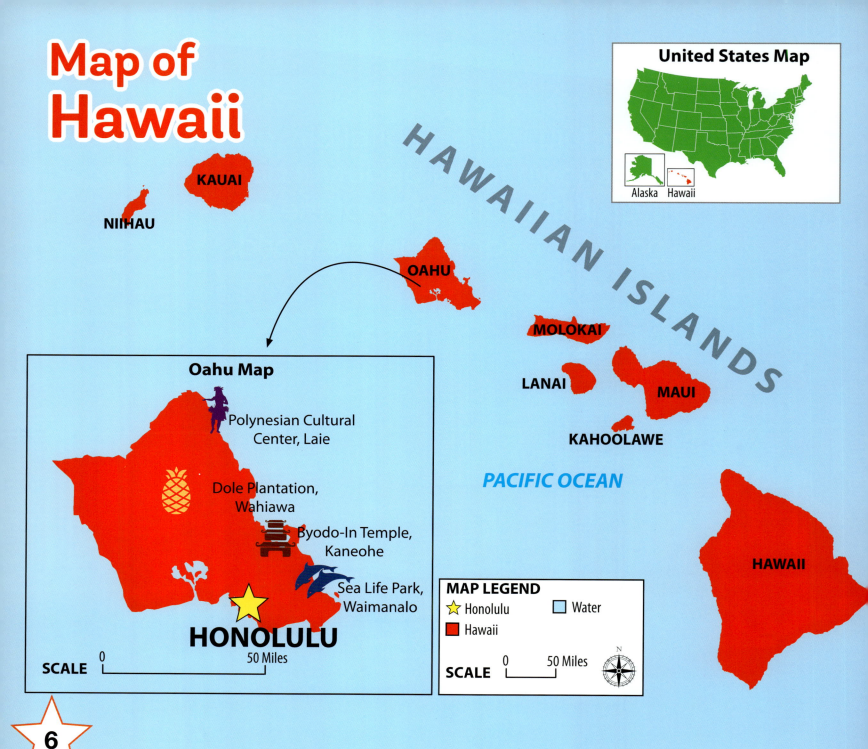

Where Is Honolulu?

Honolulu is located on the island of Oahu. Oahu is one of the eight major islands that make up the state of Hawaii. The Pacific Ocean surrounds all eight islands.

There are many exciting places to visit in Oahu. You can use a road map to plan a trip. Which roads could you take from Honolulu to get to these other places? How long might it take you to get to each place?

TRAVELING HAWAII
Honolulu to Kaneohe 11 miles
Honolulu to Waimanalo 17 miles
Honolulu to Wahiawa 21 miles
Honolulu to Laie 32 miles

Climate

Honolulu is in an area called the tropics. This means that the city stays warm all year round. The Sun shines for much of the year.

The city has only two seasons. Summer lasts from May to October. Winter takes place from November to April. Honolulu receives most of its rain in the winter.

Honolulu gets about **3,000 hours** of sunshine each year.

Population and Geography

Honolulu is Hawaii's largest city. More than 350,000 people live there. It is the only city in the state with more than 100,000 people living in it.

Honolulu sits along the coast of the Pacific Ocean. The Koolau Mountains are north of the city. These mountains were formed from volcanoes. Honolulu itself is home to several old volcanoes.

Many Peoples

The Polynesians lived in the Honolulu area long before anyone else. They came to the island more than 1,500 years ago. In 1794, the first European arrived. His name was William Brown.

In 1795, a king named Kamehameha the Great took over Oahu. Honolulu later became the royal capital. People from all over the world started to come to the city. In 1898, it became part of the United States.

Honolulu is home to the **only royal palace** in the United States.

Tourism

Most visitors to Honolulu come to spend time in the ocean. Many people come to surf the waters. Some want to take a boat tour. Other people like to sit on the beach and watch the waves.

Diamond Head is another popular place to visit. This mountain used to be a volcano. People who go to the top can get a great view of the ocean and city below.

About **2,500 people** hike to the top of **Diamond Head** every day.

Sports

Honolulu's main sports teams play for the University of Hawaii. The school has teams in several sports. These include football and volleyball. All of the men's teams are called the Rainbow Warriors. The women's teams are called the Rainbow Wahine.

The Honolulu Marathon takes place every December. It is one of the world's largest foot races. People come from all over the world to run in it.

Economy

Tourism is the top industry in Honolulu. Every year, millions of people visit the city. They stay in hotels, eat at restaurants, and buy souvenirs.

Growing food also brings money to the city. Pineapples and bananas are both grown in the area. These foods are sold to countries around the world.

More than **5.9 million** tourists visited Honolulu in **2018**.

Honolulu Timeline

1,500 years ago
Polynesians live in the Honolulu area.

1809
King Kamehameha the Great makes Honolulu his home.

1850
Honolulu becomes the capital of Hawaii.

1898
Honolulu and the rest of Hawaii become a U.S. territory.

1901 The Moana, Honolulu's first hotel, opens.

1907 The University of Hawaii is founded.

1941 Japanese forces attack Pearl Harbor, a U.S. Navy base west of Honolulu.

2019 Honolulu is voted the most livable city in the United States.

Things to Do in Honolulu

Manoa Falls
This 150-foot waterfall is located in the north part of the city. It is at the end of a 1.5-mile hiking trail through the rainforest.

Honolulu Zoo
More than 1,200 animals live at the Honolulu Zoo. Some of them, such as the Nene goose, are unique to Hawaii.

Iolani Palace
Completed in 1882, the royal palace has 10 rooms open to the public. They include the Throne Room, Grand Hall, and King's Library.

Bishop Museum
This museum has many items linked to Hawaii's past. Visitors can see King Kamehameha's cape and a fishing canoe.

Pearl Harbor National Memorial
Built in remembrance of the Japanese attack, this memorial takes visitors through the events of that day.

KEY WORDS

Research has shown that as much as 65 percent of all written material published in English is made up of 300 words. These 300 words cannot be taught using pictures or learned by sounding them out. They must be recognized by sight. This book contains 108 common sight words to help young readers improve their reading fluency and comprehension. This book also teaches young readers several important content words, such as proper nouns. These words are paired with pictures to aid in learning and improve understanding.

Page	Sight Words First Appearance
4	get, know, to
5	city, for, in, is, it, its, most, of, one, the, world
7	a, all, are, can, could, each, from, how, long, make, many, might, on, other, places, state, take, that, there, these, up, use, where, which, you
8	about, an, has, lasts, means, much, only, this, two, year
11	along, and, home, live, more, mountains, old, people, than, were, with
12	before, came, come, first, great, his, later, name, over, part, started, they, took, was
15	another, be, below, day, every, go, like, some, time, want, watch, waters, who
16	men, play, run, school
19	also, around, at, both, eat, food
21	opens
22	animals, as, do, end, mile, such, them, things, through
23	see

Page	Content Words First Appearance
4	Honolulu
5	beaches, Hawaii, Waikiki Beach
7	island, map, Oahu, Pacific Ocean, roads, trip
8	April, area, climate, hours, May, November, October, rain, seasons, summer, Sun, sunshine, tropics, winter
11	coast, geography, Koolau Mountains, population, volcanoes
12	capital, European, Kamehameha, king, palace, Polynesians, United States, William Brown
15	Diamond Head, top, tour, tourism, view, visitors, waves
16	December, football, Honolulu Marathon, races, Rainbow Wahine, Rainbow Warriors, sports, teams, University of Hawaii, volleyball
19	bananas, countries, economy, hotels, industry, money, pineapples, restaurants, souvenirs, tourists
20	territory, timeline
21	forces, Moana, Navy base, Pearl Harbor
22	Honolulu Zoo, Manoa Falls, Nene goose, rainforest, trail, waterfall
23	attack, Bishop Museum, canoe, cape, events, Grand Hall, Iolani Palace, items, King's Library, past, Pearl Harbor National Memorial, public, rooms, Throne Room

Published by AV2
350 5th Avenue, 59th Floor New York, NY 10118
Website: www.av2books.com

Copyright ©2021 AV2
All rights reserved. No part of this publication may be reproduced, stored in a retrieval system, or transmitted in any form or by any means, electronic, mechanical, photocopying, recording, or otherwise, without the prior written permission of the publisher.

Library of Congress Control Number: 2019039033

ISBN 978-1-7911-1598-2 (hardcover)
ISBN 978-1-7911-1599-9 (softcover)
ISBN 978-1-7911-1600-2 (multi-user eBook)
ISBN 978-1-7911-1601-9 (single-user eBook)

Printed in Guangzhou, China
1 2 3 4 5 6 7 8 9 0 24 23 22 21 20

012020
100919

Project Coordinator: Heather Kissock   Designer: Ana María Vidal

AV2 acknowledges Getty Images, Alamy, Newscom, Shutterstock, and Wikimedia as the primary image suppliers for this title.